CHRISTMAS AT HOME

Homemade Holiday Gift Ideas

Rebecca Germany

BARBOUR BOOKS
An Imprint of Barbour Publishing, Inc.

Published by Barbour Books, an imprint of Barbour Publishing, Inc., P.O. Box 719, Uhrichsville, Ohio 44683, www.barbourbooks.com

Member of the
Evangelical Christian
Publishers Association

Printed in Canada.

Contents

Simply Special Gifts 5

Kid-Involved Gifts 46

Homemade Decorations to Share 69

From the Kitchen 96

Gift Bundles 145

The Wrap Up 152

L ike the wise men, we give because the Lord first gave to us. The homemade touch puts an extra special quality on any gift. Going the homemade route can save money, and it doesn't have to take lots of time. The best gifts, though, aren't those with high price tag or those at the top of the popularity list. They are the ones that come from the heart.

> *"There are no great things, only small things with great love. Happy are those."*
>
> MOTHER TERESA

Simply Special Gifts

"Freely you have received, freely give."

MATTHEW 10:8

Memory Books

These are perfect gifts for the hard-to-buy-for relative. Purchase a small blank journal or autograph book and write down some special, funny, and heartwarming memories about the person you will give it to. If time allows, pass the book around to other relatives and friends, and have them contribute a short note. Embellish pages with stickers, drawings, small photos, and the like. It is sure to be a gift that will be cherished for years to come.

Family History Book

Put your computer to work. Scan old family photos. Get as many pictures of grandparents and notable relatives as you can find—showing them young and old. Arrange the pictures on pages, starting with the oldest, and type an explanation of who the person was, when and where they lived, and any unique information you can provide about them. Use the photos and descriptions to trace family history and pass on important family notes about faith, traditions, and health. Print the pages on paper with some weight and durability. Use a three-hole punch and bind the pages in a small, ringed binder, or have a print shop bind your booklet. Make multiple copies so each individual in the family has one.

Family Cookbook

Organize your recipe box and create a special gift in the process. Take all those old handwritten recipe cards, newspaper clippings, and flagged cookbooks, and type the recipes into your computer. Be sure to include a note with each recipe that states who made it stand out and how it became a family favorite. If you have a handwritten recipe from a special relative who is now deceased, you may want to photocopy or scan it to preserve the handwriting as a piece of history. You can even divide your recipes according to the cooks and include their pictures. Place the pages on durable paper and bind them in a ringed binder that can be added to as more recipes become family treasures.

Personal Touch Calendar

Take a store-bought calendar and add family birthdays, anniversaries, and events for a new family member. Or, use your computer to create your own calendar. Insert family pictures on special dates.

Family Photos

It sounds too easy and even a bit egotistical, but distant (and not-so-distant) relatives and friends love to receive pictures of you and your growing family. You don't have to go to the expense of a professional portrait. A good snapshot with a pretty background will do fine. Buy an inexpensive frame for it. Or, collect several snapshots from special occasions throughout the year and put together a small photo album.

Growth Chart

A tape measure
2 dowel rods ¼" to ½" in diameter and 18" long
1½ yds of plain fabric
A piece of nursery fabric with patterns that can be cut out
Fusible webbing

Cut the fabric 18 inches wide and 1½ yards long. Make a deep hem in the top and bottom of the fabric, leaving an opening to slip the dowels through. Sew the tape measure onto the fabric starting with the (1) at the bottom of the fabric and going straight up. Cut shapes and patterns from the printed fabric and iron them onto the plain fabric with fusible webbing. You might use fabric paint to put the child's name across the top. Insert dowels. Tie a length of string snuggly onto the ends of the top dowel for a hanger. When hung, the bottom of the tape measure will need to be even with the floor.

Name Plaque

Try your hand at calligraphy (or use your computer's fancy fonts), and write the recipient's name on special paper. (Find some with weight that's light in color—perhaps with pressed flowers in the grain or another subtle design.) Add the meaning of the name or a thoughtful poem. You could use your child's name and add his or her handprints as a great gift for grandparents.

The Personalized Touch

With a little fabric paint and/or stitching, the following items could be personalized with the recipient's name or a unique design. Add embellishments like sequins and buttons for an extra-special touch.

Aprons
Doormat
Gloves
Napkins
Pillowcases

Placemats
Potholders
T-shirts and sweatshirts
Tennis shoes
Towels

Personalized Pillowcase

Use muslin to make a simple case, or buy an inexpensive case. Place a sturdy piece of cardboard inside the case and use a pencil to lightly mark your design. Use fabric paint pens or permanent markers to create a colorful, personalized design. Write the recipient's name, a Bible verse, or blessing on the pillowcase and create simple flowers, vines, or shapes for decoration.

Personalized Scripture Cards

From Lena Nelson Dooley of Hurst, TX

"For I know the plans I have for you, Rebecca," declares the Lord,
"plans to prosper you and not to harm you,
plans to give you hope and a future."

JEREMIAH 29:11

Choose several Scriptures in which a name can be appropriately added. Write them on cards, or set them up with a computer and printer. Use small, uniform-sized cards that can be bundled with ribbon. For computer printing, try a sheet of business cards that are perforated for easy separation.

Fabric Button Earrings

From a fabric store, buy a kit for fabric-covered buttons. From a craft store, buy earring backs. Use scraps of pretty calico or a fancy but sturdy (though not thick) fabric. Follow the kit's instructions for making the button cover. Twist off the button loop with pliers. Glue the earring back to the center of the button's back with a heavy craft glue.

Simple Homemade Soap

A mold (specially bought plastic
    soap mold, cookie cutters,
    or even an ice cube tray)
Bar soap remains (mild soap
    like Ivory works well)

Grater
Water
Food coloring
Perfume or potpourri oil

Grate soap pieces into a powdery texture. Mix with just enough water
to create a thick paste. Add a drop or two of food coloring and fragrance. Knead the mixture until it is thick like dough; press the mixture
into a mold, or roll the soap into balls. Let it dry for at least 24 hours.
For a simple gift, tie a ribbon around the homemade bars of soap or
fill a small gift basket with little soap shapes.

Bath Bombs

In a glass bowl, mix 1 part citric acid (you can get this at a pharmacy) with 2¼ parts baking soda. Add several drops of essential oil and a few drops of food coloring. Moisten by spraying with water or witch hazel (witch hazel works better because it evaporates more quickly) until mixture just begins to stick together. Shape truffle-sized balls (1-inch diameter) of the mixture. Let the bombs dry and harden for 24–48 hours. Pack each bomb into its own paper candy cup. Store bombs in a closed container. To use, drop 1–3 into warm bath water.

Scented Bath Salts

2 c Epsom's salts
1 c sea salt, rock salt,
   or coarse salt
Food coloring
   (green or blue, optional)

¼ tsp glycerin
4 or 5 drops essential oil
   for fragrance (vanilla,
   citrus, or peppermint)

Combine salts in a large glass or metal mixing bowl and mix well. Add food coloring, a few drops at a time, until desired color is achieved. For white salts, simply skip the coloring. Add glycerin and essential oil and mix well. Spoon salts into clean, dry jars with cork stoppers or metal screw-on lids and seal. Makes 3 cups of bath salts. When giving as a gift, attach a label identifying the scent and recommend using ⅓ to ½ cup in the bath.

Milk Bath Powder

1 c dry milk
5–8 drops scented oil (perfume oil or essential oil)

Combine dry milk with oil and mix well. The more oil used, the stronger the scent. Place in a pretty jar. Attach a card with directions: To use, add to running bath water. You'll come out soft and smelling good!

Rose Water

3 c rose petals,
    picked just after the morning dew has dried
3 c purified water

Place petals in a glass container and pour boiling water over the petals. Allow to steep for 2 days, stirring frequently. Strain. Pour into pretty bottles; seal, and give with a pretty identification card and ribbon attached.

Peppermint Skin Toner

1 pt vinegar
1 pt purified water

1 c mint leaves

Place all ingredients in a glass saucepan and bring to a boil. Remove from heat. Pour into a glass jar and allow to steep for 4 days. Strain and bottle in decorative containers. Label each container with a pretty identification card and ribbon.

Sinus Headache Pillows

flax seeds
crushed spearmint leaves
crushed peppermint leaves
whole lavender buds

eucalyptus leaves
rosemary leaves
$\frac{1}{8}$ yd cotton fabric

Blend the herbs. Cut two pieces of fabric 4x10 inches and sew right sides together with a $\frac{1}{4}$-inch seam. Leave a 2-inch opening. Turn it right side out and stuff with the herb mixture. Sew opening closed. Tie a ribbon around the middle with a tag including directions to use as a reliever of headaches.

Herb Sachets

Cotton fabric cut into 4"x4" squares
1 handful each of dried lavender flowers and rosemary
1 tbsp of crushed cloves
Small pieces of dried lemon peel

Blend the herbs in a bowl. Place right sides of two fabric squares together and sew a $\frac{1}{4}$-inch seam, leaving a 1-inch opening. Turn the right sides out and stuff the square pouch with the herb mixture. Sew the opening closed. (Sew a loop of ribbon onto a few sachets so they can be hung over a clothes hanger.) Wrap several sachets together in tissue paper tied with raffia. Attach a note explaining that these should be placed in drawers, closets, and boxes to protect clothing from insects and to add freshness.

Pinecone Fire Starters

Several dry pinecones
Paraffin or old candle stubs
Candlewick
Scented oil (cinnamon, bayberry, or citrus spice)

Melt the wax in a coffee can placed in a pan of water. Add a few drops of oil to melted wax. Wrap or tie a length of wick around the top of each pinecone. Dip pinecones into melted wax several times, allowing wax to harden between dips. For gift-giving: Present them in a small basket with a note of instruction to add 2–3 pinecones to fire kindling and light the wicks.

Fragrant Draft Dodger

Buy ⅓ yard of 45-inch decorative calico. Trim it down to 38 inches long. Trim the short ends with pinking shears. On the long side, fold the right sides together and sew a ½-inch seam. Turn right side out. Gather the fabric at one end. About 3 inches in, secure with a rubber band, then fill the tube with dry potpourri. Stop about 3 inches from the end. Gather the fabric and secure with a rubber band. Tie raffia, jute, or ribbon over the rubber bands, and you're done. Place at the bottom of drafty doors.

Scented Notepaper

Plan at least one month ahead for this homemade gift. Buy fine-textured rice or petal paper. Fill a pretty gift box ¾ full of paper. Between every 3–4 sheets of paper, sprinkle a handful of flowers (freesia, lavender, orange blossom, or rose) or scented herbs. Cover the box and let it sit for 4 weeks. Remove the flowers and tie a satin ribbon around the stack of paper.

Mosaic Coaster

4" clay saucer
Small pieces of broken
   stained glass or colored tile
Heavy craft glue

1 thin sheet of cork
Acrylic paint
Tile grout

Paint the saucer—except for the bottom of the inside where the glass will be glued on. Allow paint to dry completely. Arrange pieces of glass on the bottom inside of the saucer, covering the entire area. When you have a pattern set, start gluing one piece at a time. Just a dab of glue will do. As the glue sets for about 30 minutes, prepare your grout. Spread the grout over all the glass and gently press it into the spaces between each piece. Let it set about 10 minutes; use a damp sponge to wipe extra grout from the surface of the glass and along the painted sides of the saucer. Allow the grout to dry overnight. The last step is to glue on a circle of cork that is just a bit smaller than the bottom of the saucer. As a finishing touch, you can apply a grout sealer to protect the white grout from stain.

Scented Coasters (and Trivets)

Pre-quilted material
Thread
Granulated potpourri from a paper sachet

Cut two 3–4-inch circles or squares from the pre-quilted material. Pin them together with right sides facing. Stitch them together, leaving a hole large enough to place potpourri. Turn stitched pieces right side out and press with a warm iron. Fill with potpourri. (You may want to make larger ones as trivets.) When you place a hot container or cup of tea on the coaster or trivet, the heat will activate the aroma.

Lighted Potpourri Jar

1 qt canning jar
1 string of 18–25 white
    Christmas lights

Potpourri
4"–6" lace or crocheted doily

Place the end of the light string that does not have the plug in the bottom of the jar. Add a handful of potpourri. Start winding the light string into the jar, stopping occasionally to add more potpourri. When the jar is full, let the cord with plug hang out and cover the top with the doily. Secure the doily in place by tying raffia or ribbon around the edge. When you plug this in, the low heat generated from the lights will warm the potpourri and fill the room with fragrance.

Jar Lamp

1 qt canning jar
   with lid and ring
1 small hurricane lamp shade
   with a base the same diameter
   of the jar's mouth
1 wick (the length of the jar)

1 ceramic lamp oil adapter
   available from craft stores
   with candle-making
   supplies
Clear lamp oil
Large pieces of potpourri

First, poke a hole in the center of the jar lid and set the adapter over the hole. Thread the wick through both holes. Fill a clean, dry jar with large pieces of potpourri (like dry orange slices, cinnamon sticks, pinecones, and whole cloves). Cover the contents completely with lamp oil. Set the lid on the jar, carefully pushing the wick down into the oil and potpourri. Tighten the ring down on the lid and set the hurricane shade in place.

Shaded Lamp

Buy an inexpensive lamp with a plain white shade. Use acrylic paints to stencil a design onto the shade. Or sponge-paint the shade, using 3 blending colors.

Umbrella Holder

Gather 3 three-pound coffee cans. Clean them and cut out the bottoms. Set the cans on top of each other and glue or solder the edges together. Measure the perimeter of a can and the height of the stack; then cut fabric for covering the cans completely. You can stitch cloth shapes onto the fabric for design. Use thick glue to attach the fabric to the cans.

Coffee Can Canisters

Collect 1- and 2-pound sizes of coffee cans with lids. Spray, brush-paint, or sponge-paint with enamel. Allow the paint to dry completely. Add decals, ribbon edges, and other designs that fit snug and flat against the can. Paint the words "flour," "sugar," and "salt" on the cans, if desired. Add several coats of clear spray coating so the canisters can be wiped clean.

Cheese Board

Buy a very smooth, nice piece of maple wood, 1-inch thick and 8–10 inches wide. Cut it into a square and sand the rough edges. Seal with varathane or other sealant. Give with a cheese knife or slicer.

Decorative Curtain
Any teen will enjoy this fun gift.

1 yardstick
1 big bag of neon-colored
   drinking straws

1 bag of colorful beads
1 skein of yarn

Take a yardstick (often given away by lumber companies) and drill a
hole at every inch marker. Drill against a piece of scrap lumber to keep
the yardstick from cracking. Paint the yardstick, then cut the yarn in
5–6-foot lengths, and tie one end of each length through a hole in the
yardstick. Cut the straws in thirds (about 2 inches per section) and
thread them onto the yarn. Add a bead (or even a fake flower) every so
often. When you reach the bottom of the yarn, secure a large bead for
weight. When done, the curtain should fit across the average doorway.

Exercise Mat

2 terrycloth beach towels (approximately 28"x 49")
A sheet of thick foam from a fabric or upholstery store cut 2"
    smaller than the size of one towel
2 elastic strips 30" long and 2" wide

Pin the towels together and stitch a ¼-inch seam, leaving an opening
of at least 6 inches. Trim the corners and turn right sides out. Insert
the foam. Hand-stitch the opening closed. For each piece of elastic,
sew the ends together to make a circle. Use these elastic circles to slip
over the mat when it is rolled.

Heating Bag

*This little bag is very nice for soothing
little aches and pains or warming cold feet.*

½ yd of flannel (cotton) fabric
18" of 1" wide
    cotton webbing, cut into 2
    equal pieces

4 c uncooked rice
1 tbsp whole cloves

Cut the flannel into a 14x18-inch rectangle. Fold, right sides facing, to 7x18 inches. Mark each short end at the fold with a straight pin; unfold. For handles: Pin one end of webbing 1 inch from the fold; pin remaining end 1¾ inches from the cut edge. Repeat for opposite handle on other short end. Fold fabric in half, right sides facing with handles sandwiched inside. Pin the edges allowing a ¾-inch seam, and sew the bag together, leaving a 3-inch opening along the long side. Clip the corners and turn the bag right side out. Fill with rice and cloves, then hand-sew the opening closed. To use as a heating pad, microwave for 1–2 minutes on high. Remove from microwave, using the handles.

A Living Gift

Give a gift of a homegrown houseplant (or herbs you've cultivated from seeds). Take clippings from a hearty plant like an ivy, philodendron, or spider plant. Start them in a tin, a clay pot, a coffee mug, an old boot, a lined basket, or any unique pot. Keep soil moist until rooted. Attach plant care instructions with a ribbon.

Blossoming Bucket

Buy some spring bulbs for daffodils, tulips, or hyacinths, and put them in the coldest corner of your refrigerator for 2–4 weeks. Fill over half a bucket or large vase with gravel, pebbles, or marbles. Nestle the bulbs among the top pebbles, points facing upward. Add water just to the top of the pebbles. In a few weeks there will be blossoms for all to enjoy. Give the bucket away at any stage of the bulbs' growth.

Sweet Treats

Fill a canning jar with colorful candies. Tie a ribbon and tag around the neck of the jar, and you have an instant gift. Add a note tag that says "You are a real sweetie" or "I appreciate your sweet friendship." A jar could also be filled with small cookie cutters. Attach your favorite sugar cookie recipe.

Give Old Things New Life

- Old windows become mirrors. Just replace the glass panes with some mirrors cut to size by a glass shop.

- Torn or stained quilts can be remade into stuffed toys, small pillows, framed artwork, etc.

- Remove crystal drops from a broken or incomplete chandelier and use as tree ornaments.

- Put old doorknobs or drawer pulls in a line on a stained and varnished or painted board for a unique pegboard on which to hang coats or other items.

- Put a simple wooden top and base on a thick old porch or stair spindle and create a stand for a plant or lamp.

- Melt old candle stubs. Fill an old teacup or seashell with wax and wick.

- Any kind of container that has lost its lid—cookie jar, teapot, candy dish, etc.—can become a unique flowerpot.

- Old house shutters attached together with hinges can have new life. Use tall ones for a room divider and short ones for a fireplace screen.

Incredible Clay

¼ c household glue
⅓ c cornstarch

Dab of acrylic paint
(optional)

Make clay by mixing glue with cornstarch. Add a drop of paint if you want to color your clay. Stir together until flaky, then knead with hands until it turns to a smooth clay consistency. (Store clay in an airtight bag until ready to use.) Roll out clay with a rolling pin until it is ⅛-inch thick. Cut out shapes with cookie cutters, if desired, then let dry overnight. While clay is still damp, you can mold the shape and glue it against a picture frame or decorative can. You can also let the rolled-out clay dry out overnight and cut out shapes with scissors. Decorate with acrylic paints or permanent markers either while damp or when dry. It is incredibly versatile clay.

Kid's Dress-Up Chest

Buy a large, plastic storage box with lid. Paint the sides with fabric or acrylic paints. Use the child's name in your design. Then go to yard sales and thrift shops, collecting several pieces of unique clothing—like a wedding dress and veil, prom dresses, ballerina's tutu, uniforms, costumes, and the like. Also look for extravagant hats, shoes, purses, and jewelry. Fill the storage box, and give the gift of hours of imaginative fun.

Kid-Involved Gifts

*"It is good to be children sometimes,
and never better than at Christmas,
when its mighty Founder was a child Himself."*

A CHRISTMAS CAROL, CHARLES DICKENS

*"If you, then, though you are evil,
know how to give good gifts to your children,
how much more will your Father in heaven
give good gifts to those who ask him!"*

MATTHEW 7:11

A Special Bookmark

This one's sure to please Grandma and Grandpa! Gather old and new pictures of your family and trim them to fit on a piece of heavy paper that is approximately 2x7 inches. Arrange them on the front and back and secure in place with glue. You can add the date, a Scripture, or sentiment, etc. Have the bookmark laminated, or cover it with clear contact paper.

Photo Puzzle Cards

Get a large print made of a favorite family photo. Mount the photo to green or red poster board with spray adhesive or a light, even coating of glue. When dry, write a greeting on the backside. Help the child use scissors to cut the photo into 8–12 pieces. Place in an envelope and mail. (You may want to place the puzzle in a small plastic bag before placing it in the envelope.)

Puzzle Picture Frame

Pick up an old jigsaw puzzle or two from a garage sale (the more colorful the pieces the better). Fashion a square, triangle, or hexagon out of craft sticks by gluing them together. Then glue the jigsaw pieces on the sticks. Make a wide frame with enough space in the middle to attach a picture to the back. Cut out lightweight cardboard in the same size and shape as the stick frame, and glue it behind the picture. Attach string or ribbon to hang this ornament to your tree or a magnet for refrigerator displays. (Hot glue makes the project quick but requires supervision when children are involved.)

Silhouette Picture

Gather a flashlight, a large piece of heavy white paper, and a pen, pencil, or marker. Tape the paper to the wall. Have your child stand or sit sideways beside the paper. Darken the room and shine the flashlight on the child so the profile is shadowed on the paper. Trace the shadow; then cut out the profile and mount it on a contrasting piece of paper. This is striking with the profile cut out of black paper and mounted on white paper or vice versa.

Plaster Handprint

In a large disposable container, mix together 1 cup of water and $2\frac{1}{4}$ cups of plaster of paris until it is thick but pourable. Pour into an aluminum pie plate. When the plaster is firm enough to hold a shape, have the child press his or her hand into it and carefully lift up. Allow the child to press some marbles, seashells, or other small embellishments into the plaster, but leave the handprint untouched. Let the mold dry completely overnight. Record the date and the child's name on back.

Personalized T-Shirt

This needs adult supervision. Gather crayon shavings and bits, and place them in an emptied and cleaned soup can. (You will need a different can for each color used). Place the can over a pan of boiling water until crayon is melted. Work quickly to paint pictures and words on a plain cotton T-shirt, apron, or glove (with cardboard protection underneath or between fabric layers). For permanent color, cover the design with a scrap of fabric or old towel and press with a hot iron.

No Skidding Socks

Buy a quality pair of thick socks. Trace the foot of the person you will give the socks to (or use the foot of someone of similar size) onto cardboard. Put the cardboard foot shape into the sock, then use fabric paint to decorate the bottom of the sock. When the paint is completely dry, put the sock in the dryer for 10–15 minutes in order to set the paint.

Scented Sachet

Cut a circle of lightweight fabric 8–10 inches in diameter. In the center, pile either rose petals; cotton balls with vanilla oil; cinnamon bark with orange peels and cloves; lemon thyme and lemon verbena leaves; or lavender flowers. Draw up the edge and tie with ribbon.

Fragrant Soap Balls

Ivory Snow Flakes   Perfume or scented oil
Food coloring

Use water to moisten the soap flakes to a consistency likened to very stiff dough. Divide the mixture into several bowls. Add a different perfume and food coloring to each bowl for variety. Have children shape large spoonfuls of the soap into balls. Place the balls on trays (labeled with their molder's name!) to harden for several days. Have each child wrap his or her soap balls in colored cellophane paper and tie the package with a pretty ribbon.

Quilted Pillows

For a good way to get children to learn simple sewing skills try this: Gather fabric scraps (preferably cotton) and cut 9 squares, approximately 4x4 inches. Help your child sew the pieces together by hand to form one 12x12-inch square (for younger children you might want to use only 4 squares that are 6x6 inches so there is less sewing to do). For the backside you can do another set of 9 squares, or you can choose one piece of fabric that measures 12x12 inches. Place both 12-inch square pieces with right sides facing and sew around the edges, leaving a small section open to flip it right side out. Fill with polyester stuffing and sew up the opening.

Decorative Light Switch Cover

Gather 9 Popsicle sticks (the amount used can vary with size of light cover), craft glue, a sheet of craft foam, and foam craft shapes. Use the existing light cover to cut the foam sheet to fit the switch area. Mark the center opening with a pen and use a utility knife to cut an opening in the center of the foam. Place one stick against the switch and mark where to cut the opening. An adult should help with the sharp scissors or a utility knife to cut the stick. Glue the sticks onto the foam, straight and touching. The sticks should hang over the edges of the foam just a bit to cover it. Decorate the switch cover with paint and foam shapes. When the switch cover is completely dry, use double-sided tape to attach it to the existing switch plate cover.

Glass Aquarium

Glass container   Artificial greenery
Glass fish with floats   Sand or decorative gravel
Shells, stones, or marbles

Select a fish bowl, a regular bowl, or a decorative bottle or jar for your
aquarium. If you choose a glass container with a lid, it will require less
cleaning and the water will not evaporate as quickly. Start with some
sand or gravel on the bottom and anchor your greenery into it. Add
some seashells or glass marbles for interest. Slowly pour water into the
aquarium (you can color the water with food coloring), then add the
floating glass fish.

CD Coaster

4–6 CDs (plain gold or
silver CDs look best)

White cotton lace
Glue

Hold a CD in one hand and spread some glue along the outside edge.
Take one end of the lace (don't cut it yet) and lay it along the glued
edge, pleating it as you go. When you've gone all around, cut the lace
to meet the starting end. The coaster is done and will hold heat well.

Pretzel Wreath

Use small pretzels (those that are almost heart shaped). Arrange one layer of them in a circle like a wreath, then glue a second layer on top of the first, joining the pretzels together over the middle of a pretzel on the first layer. Weave ribbon between the holes if you like. Hang with a ribbon.

Scoop of Hugs and Kisses

Laundry soap scoop
Hugs and Kisses candy

Clear or colored plastic wrap
Ribbon

Fill the scoop with candy. Cut a large piece of plastic wrap and place the scoop in the middle. Draw the plastic wrap tightly around the scoop and gather it around the handle. Tie a ribbon around the handle to hold the wrap in place. Add a note that says, "Hugs and Kisses from me to you."

Pet Rock Paperweight

Glue two well-shaped rocks together to make the head and body of a duck, ladybug, or other creature. Add features with markers, bits of felt or fabric, pipe cleaners, wiggly eyes, and so on.

Snow Globe

Clean a glass jar that has a lid. (Small jam or peanut butter jars work well, but avoid the ones with the "fresh test button" on the lid.) Fill the jar with water, screw on the lid, and turn it upside down for awhile to see if the seal will hold water. Paint the outside of the lid with a coat or two of acrylic paint. Arrange a grouping of clean plastic (or otherwise waterproof) items on the inside of the lid. Glue them in place with a water-resistant glue. When the glue has dried, fill the jar with water and add approximately a teaspoon of gold or silver glitter. Put a tiny ribbon of glue around the inside edge of the lid and immediately screw the lid tightly onto the jar.

Glove Puppets

Buy inexpensive ladies' knit gloves. For each glove, gather 5 1-inch pompoms and 10 5-millimeter wiggle eyes. You'll also need thick craft glue and 5 tongue depressors. Each pompom will be a head. First glue the eyes in place. A tiny pompom or sequin can be added for a nose. Ears made of felt can be glued to the back. Be creative with embellishments. Before putting the head onto the end of the glove finger, insert a tongue depressor inside the finger and allow the glue to set before removing the stick.

Spoon Puppets

Gather wooden spoons and embellishments like 7-millimeter wiggle eyes, foam shapes, fabric and ribbon remnants, paint, and markers, including hot or craft glue. Start by painting your spoon. The back of the spoon will be the face area. You may want flesh color above where the spoon narrows to the handle and a bright color along the handle. Set eyes in place with glue. Use a sharp permanent marker to add a smile. Cut small circles out of foam for cheeks, nose, and ears. Glue in place. Tie ribbon to the "neck." Use thin strips of fabric or ribbon for "hair." Be creative.

To make a snowman: Paint your spoon all white. Set eyes in place. Use a long teardrop-shaped orange foam piece for nose and small circles of foam in red or pink for cheeks. Paint a 2-inch straw hat black and add a holiday ribbon to the neck for a scarf.

Turtle Trinket Box

2 clay saucers, 4" in diameter   Small foam ball
4 clay pots 1½" tall   2 wiggle eyes

Paint the saucers and pots with acrylic paint (green is great for this project). You can add a shell design to one saucer that will be used on the top side of the turtle's shell. Paint some toes on the clay pots on the outside edges with the opening facing down. Paint the foam ball, adding face detail as you like. Allow the paint to dry. Use heavy craft glue to attach the foam ball to the saucer that will be the top, face-down. Place the bottom saucer facedown on your table, then glue the bottom of the pots to the bottom of the saucer. When dry, place the rims of the saucers together. The top lifts off when you are ready to place trinkets inside.

Decoupaged Bottles

Colorful tissue paper
White glue
Paintbrush

Clean, clear glass or plastic
bottles, jars, vases, or
bowls

Make sure whatever you are decoupaging is clean, dry, and dust-free.
Rip or cut tissue paper into different shapes. Water down the glue just
a bit. Brush glue on small areas of object you are decoupaging. Place
colored tissue in desired pattern. Paint a little more glue on top of tissue. Let dry. It's best to work on a protected surface. Place gifts like a
candle, bath salts, or homemade potpourri inside the finished bottles.

"Most Special" Gift Box

Paint or cover the outside of a shoebox with paper and decorate. Keep the lid separate and removable. Secure a small mirror onto the bottom of the inside of the box. Make a card that reads something like "The person pictured here is one of the most special gifts in my life." Glue it on the inside of the box top.

Homemade
Decorations
to Share

"We will share with you whatever good things the Lord gives us."

Numbers 10:32

Fabric Garland

Scraps of cotton Christmas   Twine, jute, or heavy string
fabric and even some plain
colors and muslin

Cut a length of twine at least 6 feet long. Tie a loop in one end. Cut fabric in strips measuring 1x6 inches. Tie the fabric onto the twine—knot in the middle and equal amount of fabric on both sides. Alternate fabrics as you go. Keep the pieces close together for a full effect to your garland.

You'll want at least 24 feet for an average 6-foot tree. You can also drape this garland across your curtain rods or around your banister.

Rag Tree

A straight twig 8–14" long and as thick as a kindergartner's pencil
A base out of a branch 1½" tall and 2" in diameter
⅛ yd of cotton fabric in Christmas color
24–36 tiny pinecones no more than a ¼" tall

Whittle the smallest end of the twig to a point. Match a drill bit to the other end of the twig and drill a hole in the base piece at least 1 inch deep. Glue the twig into the hole. Cut strips of fabric with pinking shears, ¾-inch wide by 6 inches long. Tie the first strip just below the pointed tip of the twig. Add strips, keeping them close and altering the direction the ends hang. When the twig is full, use the pinking shears to trim the ends of the fabric to vary the lengths—longest at bottom to shortest at top. Glue a small pinecone to the end of each fabric strip.

Scented Tree Ornaments

1 c applesauce
¾ c cinnamon
2 tbsp ground cloves

2 tbsp nutmeg
2 tbsp ginger

Mix all ingredients together. Roll onto waxed paper to ⅛-inch thickness. Cut out with cookie cutters. Poke holes for hangers with a drinking straw. Put on a wire rack and allow to dry for 3 days, turning daily. Use fabric paints, sequins, and other embellishments to dress them up. Makes approximately 1 dozen ornaments.

Candy-Coated Ornaments

Buy several small foam balls. Spread a coating of glue over the ball and glue on your favorite candy. Red cinnamon candies, crushed peppermint sticks, round peppermints glued on their narrow sides, gumdrops, M&Ms, or any other fun candy will work (best to use just one variety of candy per ball). Use a long straight pin to secure a loop of ribbon to the top for a hanger.

Cookie Cutter Photo Ornaments

Trim a favorite photo to fit inside a cookie cutter shape. Glue the edges of the picture to the inside of the cutter. You can add ribbon, lace, glitter, and paint to the cutter as desired. Remember to label the picture with name and date. Hang on the tree. Make a collection of these ornaments to show the growth of a child or changes in the family's appearance over the years. (A great gift for Grandma!)

Fabric-Fused Wooden Ornaments

From a craft store, buy simple wooden shapes cut from ⅛-inch plywood (stars, trees, bells, etc.). Sand the rough edges and wipe them clean. Lay an old towel or sheet over your ironing board. Spread a large piece of holiday fabric (cotton) out on the ironing board face down. Place a matching-sized sheet of fusible web on it with paper side up. Cover with a thin towel and use a hot iron to press the webbing on according to the directions. When cool, peel the paper away. Set your wooden shapes on the covered ironing board. Keep them close together (about ½-inch apart). Lay the fabric over them with web side against the wood. Cover the fabric with a thin towel, and use the iron to fuse the fabric to the wood. Next, place the piece of fabric face down on a cutting board, and use a utility knife to cut around the wood shapes. Touch loose fabric with a dot of glue. Add embellishments like tiny wooden stars or buttons. Paint a name on either the fabric or wooden side. The back side can be left plain, painted, or fused with fabric. Lastly, use a tiny bit to drill a hole in the top of the ornament. Hang by gold thread or floss.

Sparkling Ornaments

Trace cookie cutter shapes onto plain paper. Place waxed paper over the design and outline it with glue. Coat the surface of the shape with glue and fill it with glitter (the ultra-fine variety works best). Let dry for several days. Cut out the shape and repeat glue and glitter on the reverse side. When completely dry, make a hole in the top and create a hanger with thread or thin ribbon.

Elegant Crèche Ornament

1 Styrofoam ball
Paint
Short pins
Sequins
2 sizes of small beads

1 tiny plastic baby
2"x2" piece of white flannel
Heavy craft glue
Thread, string, or ribbon
   for a hanger

Hollow out a place in the middle of the foam ball. If so desired, paint the ball silver or gold. Starting with a small section, smooth on a thin layer of glue onto a pin, then one of the smallest beads, followed by the larger bead and a sequin. Stick the pin into the ball. Place beaded pins all around the ball, except for in the hollowed area. At the top, choose a place to anchor your hanger with a pin. In the area not covered by pins, spread a thin amount of glue, then sprinkle a generous amount of glitter to cover it. (Do this over a pan to catch the extra glitter.) Fold the flannel around the baby and secure with glue. Then glue the baby into the hollow of your ball. You can make a tiny bow to place at the top of the hollowed area.

Charming Ball Ornaments

Buy several clear glass ball ornaments. Each one can be made to look unique and special. Remove the metal hanger from the neck of the ball to reveal an opening. Decorate the inside, then replace the hanger.

BEACH BALL: Fill the ornament with tiny seashells and coral. Add a bit of sand.

FLOWER BALL: Take apart some colorful silk flowers and stuff them down the neck of the ornament. Cut a hole in a small doily and slip over the neck on the outside. Replace the hanger and tie a ribbon around it.

MARBLED PAINT BALL: Place a drop or two of paint inside the ornament and swirl it around to coat the inside, or try using a straw inserted into the neck of the ornament to blow the paint around. Use more than one color, either at the same time or with time in between for each color to dry. Paint should be thick enough to stick to the glass, but not so thick that it globs.

NATURE BALL: Fill ⅓ of the ball with birdseed. Replace the hanger. Glue a little bit of artificial pine, a cinnamon stick branch, and a tiny mushroom bird to the neck of the ball.

PHOTO BALL: Cut a picture into a circle to fit the clear ball. Place the front inside against the glass. Stuff colored tinsel in behind the picture to hold it in place.

POPCORN BALL: Place 15–25 kernels of microwave popcorn (wiped clean of excess oils) inside the ball. Place the ornament in a paper bag and put in the microwave for 1–2 minutes (no metal). Listen carefully for the last pop; you may not need to leave the ornament in for the full time. When done popping, carefully remove the hot ornament. Sprinkle some glitter inside on the popcorn. Replace the hanger and tie a pretty ribbon around the neck.

POTPOURRI BALL: Use small pieces of potpourri to fill the ball. Hang it on your tree next to a light to warm up the potpourri and release the scent.

SAND ART BALL: Fill with layers of different colored sand.

WINTER SCENE BALL: Place very tiny pinecones in the ball and add artificial snowflakes.

Candy Train Engine
A great ornament or place favor.

Glue a roll of ring-shaped candy to the wide side of a package of gum. Glue 4 round peppermint candies to the bottom against the gum pack for wheels. Make a loop of narrow ribbon and glue the ends to the top of one end of the candy roll. Glue a caramel on top of the ribbon ends for an engineer's cab. To the other end of the candy roll, glue a chocolate kiss for a smokestack and another kiss on the same end of the package of gum for a plow front.

Queen Anne's Lace Snowflakes

Several heads of Queen Anne's lace (a wildflower/weed found
    growing along roads, in fields, and in many backyards. The plants
    have big heads, which are clusters of tiny white flowers. They
    have a lacy look and 2–3' stalks.)
Spray snow
Clear acrylic spray paint
Thin gold cord
Hot glue and gun

This project could take 1–2 weeks to complete. First, cut the plant stalks
a couple of inches below the heads. Gently rinse the heads under water
(head facing down) and place on paper towel to dry. Trim the stem very
close to the head. Lay heads on paper towels and carefully press flat.

Cover with more paper towel and place between heavy layers of paper as in phone books, newspapers, and catalogs. Check the flowers daily until they are just dry enough to hold the flat, lacy shape. Move them often so they don't stick to the paper. When the flowers are flat but still pliable, place them on a rack or screen and set them in an airy, though protected, place to dry for a day or two.

Make loops of the cord and glue to the back of each flower. Hang the flowers on a line outside or lay them on a protected surface. Spray them with snow. Apply several heavy coats, drying between. For the finishing touch spray generously with a coat of clear acrylic. A spray of glitter could also be applied.

Your snowflakes will require a gentle touch when handling.

Golden Stars

Piece of metal window screen   Gold fabric paint
Gold spray paint   Gold thread

Spray-paint the screen and let it dry. With a sharp permanent marker, draw or trace a star shape onto the screen. Cut out using old scissors. Squeeze fabric paint from the bottle onto the rough edge, creating a solid, raised line. Lay on waxed paper to dry. When dry, check that both sides of the edge have a solid line of paint. Apply more if needed. To the center, apply a design or write a word like "joy" or a name. Use gold thread to make a hanger.

Hanging Luminaries

Gather an assortment of small glass jelly, baby food, and other jars. Make sure that they have the ridge around the top for screwing on a lid. Use a medium gauge wire approximately 12–18 inches long. For each jar, twist one end around the jar, under the ridge. Make sure it is snug. Bend the remaining end straight up from the mouth of the jar and make a loop for a hanger. Add a ribbon tie around the jar's neck. Place a votive candle in each jar and fill the remaining space around the candle's bottom with rose hips. Hang an assortment of these luminaries from your porch railing or a variety of places where a candle can burn safely.

Stockings to Stuff

Use pre-printed fabrics available for making stockings with instructions for assembly. Or you can take a piece of green or red felt and draw a stocking shape with a marker. Cut two matching pieces out with pinking shears. Place the pieces together and sew a $\frac{1}{2}$-inch seam around all but the top. If the stocking is large and will hold heavy items, go around with a second seam. You will have a rough edge around the stocking. Use ribbon, glue and glitter, rickrack, fabric paint, or other embellishments to dress up your creation. Attach a loop of cord to the top if you want to hang the stocking.

Popcorn Wreath

Cover a straw wreath with popcorn using hot glue. An average wreath will use two bags of microwave popcorn. Once the wreath is covered with the popcorn, spray-paint with gold or use a sponge to spot dab some gold highlights to the popcorn. Add a bow, some small greenery sprigs, and other frills to the top of the wreath.

Yo-Yo Wreath

Cut 8 circles (3¼ inches diameter) from green Christmas fabric. Cut 8 circles (1½ inches diameter) from poster board. Leaving the thread unknotted with a long tail hanging out, make short running stitches around the circle of fabric folding ³⁄₁₆-inch of the edge under as you go. Set your poster board circle in the center on the wrong side of the fabric, then pull the thread ends to gather the fabric circle. Tie the thread securely and trim the ends. Adjust the yo-yo so the hole is in the center. Glue a red or white button to the center hole of each yo-yo. Glue the yo-yos together by slightly overlapping the edges. Use a plastic lid or other circle as a guide as you shape the yo-yos into a circle. Glue a red bow to the top or bottom of the wreath. Make one stitch of thread through the back fabric of one yo-yo, and tie the ends in a loop for a hanger.

Metallic Wreath

Foam ring
Fake leaves removed from
    stems

Gold or silver spray paint
Hot glue

Spray-paint the foam and leaves separately. When dry, use hot glue to attach leaves to the wreath, overlapping edges. It is plain, but use your imagination and add embellishments as desired.

A Centerpiece that Grows

Cotton quilt batting
(avoid polyester)
1 dinner plate
1 tall, fat candle

¼ c sproutable chive or
lentil seed (available at a
health food store)
Plastic wrap
Water spray bottle

Cover all but the center and outer edge of the plate with a layer of batting. Spray water over the batting. Scatter the seeds on and spray with more water. Carefully tip the plate to pour off any extra water. Tightly cover the plate with plastic wrap and put it in a well-lit place, but not in direct sunlight. Spray the batting every two days. When you see the first sprouts, remove the plastic wrap. Then spray with water daily. In 10–14 days, you should have a wreath of green sprouts. Place a candle in the center. The centerpiece will need to be kept in a sunlit place and watered regularly.

Fruit Candle Cups

Hollow out apples and oranges enough to fit a votive candle inside. Create a unique grouping on a platter with greenery and other fruits and nuts.

Holiday Potpourri

4 oranges
4 lemons
½ c whole cloves

½ c whole allspice
10 cinnamon sticks, broken
10 bay leaves, crumbled

Use a vegetable peeler to peel fruit carefully. Remove only the peel and not the white pith. Cut or tear peel into 1-inch pieces. Spread peel on a pan lined with a paper towel. Place in oven at 175° or on the oven's warm setting. Dry for 1½ hours, turning occasionally. Peels should be leathery and slightly brittle. Let stand and air dry on a paper towel for 24 hours. Combine with remaining ingredients. Keep in airtight container. To use: Let stand in a room in an open container or put 1 tablespoon of potpourri into 2 cups of hot water.

Dried Fruit

APPLES—Slice ⅛–¼-inch thick, including the core. Soak in lemon juice with salt for several minutes, then pat dry. They can also be sprinkled with a fruit preserver. You may want to sprinkle them with cinnamon for fragrance. Place on a lightly greased cookie sheet. Bake in a 150° oven for 6 hours. Slices should have a leathery texture. Spray with a few coats of clear acrylic.

ORANGES OR LEMONS—On a whole orange, use a knife or citrus peeler to cut approximately 6 lines down the sides and through the peel at intervals. Place on a cookie sheet and bake in a 150° oven for

10–12 hours. For slices, cut ⅛ to ¼-inch thick. Place on a lightly sprayed cookie sheet. Bake in a 150° oven for 6 hours or until edges start to curl and are pliable. Spray with a few coats of clear acrylic.

Use dried fruit on wreaths and garland, to enhance plain potpourri, or as an accent on almost anything like a gift, a picture frame, a tree ornament, and so on.

ADDITIONAL IDEA: Peel lemons and oranges, making sure to keep large sections of peel. Cut shapes in the peel with tiny cookie cutters. Allow them to air dry and add to your potpourri.

From the Kitchen

"Give, and it will be given to you.
A good measure, pressed down,
shaken together and running over,
will be poured into your lap."

LUKE 6:38

Chocolate Dipped Spoons

Plastic spoons (find festive colors)
Chocolate chips (2 oz will do about 8 spoons)
Optional flavoring extracts (almond, peppermint, anise, etc.)

Melt chips over low heat until smooth. Dip spoons up to the start of the handle, allowing a good bit of chocolate to pool in the bowl. You can sprinkle with crushed candy canes while wet, or let the spoons dry on waxed paper and drizzle white chocolate over the dark chocolate. Try dipping half of the spoon in white chocolate and half in dark. Wrap dried spoons in plastic wrap and secure with ribbon. Use as stirrers in hot coffee, cappuccino, and cocoa.

Chocolate Dipped Cookies

1 pkg sandwich cookies like Oreos or Nutter Butters
    (even homemade sugar cookies or chocolate chip cookies
    will work)
1 pkg white or chocolate almond bark
Edible sprinkle decorations (optional)

Melt almond bark in microwave or over low heat. When smooth and
hot, carefully dip cookies, one at a time, into almond bark, covering $\frac{1}{2}$
to $\frac{3}{4}$ of cookie. Place on waxed paper and shake on sprinkles.

Chocolate Dipped Candy Canes

½ c semisweet chocolate
  chips or white vanilla chips
2 tsp shortening
16 peppermint candy canes
  or sticks

Crushed, hard peppermint
  candy, red and green
  sprinkles, or miniature
  chocolate chips (optional)

Cover a cookie sheet with waxed paper. Melt chips and shortening in a saucepan over low heart until smooth. Dip ¾ of the candy cane in the chocolate. Lay on the waxed paper and allow it to cool about 2 minutes. Roll the chocolate-covered ends in decorative peppermint, sprinkles, or chips. Can be stored under loose cover for up to 2 weeks.

Candied Tea Stirrers

30–35 pieces of fruit-flavored hard candy, crushed
2 tablespoons light corn syrup
Sturdy plastic spoons

Line a cookie sheet with waxed paper and spray with cooking spray. Crush candies in a heavy plastic bag with a hammer or rolling pin. Add crushed candies to corn syrup and melt over low heat in a small saucepan. Stir often. Spoon candy into bowl of each plastic spoon. Place spoons on cookie sheet, allowing handles to rest on the raised sides so that the spoons are level. Let candy harden completely before storing in an airtight container or wrapping with plastic wrap. Use the spoons to stir and add flavor to plain hot tea.

Hard Tack Candy

1 c water
½ c light corn syrup
2 c sugar
Food coloring

½ tsp flavoring for
candy making (orange or
peppermint extract,
cinnamon oil, or other)

In a large, heavy saucepan, combine water, syrup, and sugar. Over medium heat, stir constantly until all is dissolved. Stop stirring and bring to 300° to 310°F (149° to 154°C) on a candy thermometer—or until a small amount of syrup dropped into cold water forms hard, brittle threads. Remove from heat and add flavoring and food coloring. Pour into a greased jelly roll pan and dust with powdered sugar. When cool, break into pieces. Store in airtight jars or bags.

Almond Florentines
From Denise Hunter of Fort Wayne, IN

1 c butter (margarine
will not suffice!)
1 c sugar
⅓ c honey
4 c sliced, blanched
almonds

⅓ c whipping cream
(heavy, sweet, liquid in a
carton—not aerosol or
freezer variety)
6 oz semisweet
chocolate chips

Coat 5 8-inch aluminum foil pie tins with cooking spray. Melt butter in your largest saucepan. Add sugar, honey, and cream. Bring to a boil over medium heat. Stir frequently. When the boil creates a wild froth on top, stir constantly and continue to boil at this level for exactly 90 seconds. Remove saucepan from heat. Add almonds; stir. Quickly pour mixture into the pie tins.

Bake 10–14 minutes until rich, golden brown (most likely will be bubbling). Cool in the pans for 20 minutes. Refrigerate in the pans for 30 minutes. Turn out onto waxed paper, stack in fridge with waxed paper in between. Melt chocolate and spread on the bottom of the Florentines. Let cool. Break into bark. Store in refrigerator with plastic wrap between layers.

Peppermint Bark

16 oz of either vanilla-flavored baking chips or candy coating
24 hard peppermint candies

Line a large cookie sheet with waxed paper. Place peppermint candies in a heavy plastic bag and crush with a hammer or rolling pin. Slowly melt the chips over low heat, stirring constantly until smooth. Add crushed peppermints to melted chips. Spread mixture evenly out onto cookie sheet. Let stand in cool place for at least 1 hour. Break into pieces and store in an airtight container.

Super Easy Fudge

²/₃ c evaporated milk
   (half of a regular can)
1²/₃ c sugar
¹/₂ tsp salt
1¹/₂ c mini marshmallows

1¹/₂ c baking chips in
   your choice of semisweet
   milk, or mint chocolate,
   or peanut butter
1 tsp vanilla
¹/₂ c nuts (optional)

Combine milk, sugar, and salt in a large saucepan over medium-low heat. Bring to a boil for 5 minutes, stirring constantly. Remove from heat. Add marshmallows, chips, and vanilla. Stir until smooth. Add nuts. Pour into a greased 9x9-inch pan. Refrigerate at least 1 hour until firm enough to cut. Store in an airtight container in a cool place.

Cookie Suckers

When your cookies are ready to go into the oven, press an ice cream or lollipop stick into the dough, then bake. Cool completely. Wrap them individually with clear or colored plastic wrap, and tie the wrap in place with ribbon.

Sticks and Stones Candy Mix

2 c pretzel sticks
4 c Cheerios cereal
4 c Corn Chex cereal
1 c salted peanuts
　(or mixed nuts)

1–1½ lb white almond
　bark
1–2 tsp shortening
12-oz bag of M&Ms

Melt bark with shortening over low heat. In a large bowl, combine pretzels, cereals, and nuts. Add half the melted bark to the mix and stir to coat. Add the other half and continue stirring until all is coated. Add M&Ms last and toss lightly (hot bark will cause them to melt). Spread on 2–3 waxed paper-lined cookie sheets. Refrigerate at least an hour. Break apart and store in an airtight container.

Stuffed Sugar Dates
From Wanda Royer of Scio, OH

Box of whole dates   Walnut halves (broken
White granulated sugar   in half)

Stuff each date with a piece of walnut. Roll the dates in a small bowl of sugar. Voila! Your treat is done.

Crystallized Orange Pecans

1 c sugar
¼ tsp ground cinnamon

¼ c orange juice
2–3 c pecan halves

Combine all ingredients in 2½-quart microwave-safe bowl. Cook uncovered on 70 percent power for 6 minutes (or medium power for 7–8 minutes). Stir, then resume cooking on 70 percent power for 8–10 minutes, or until crystallized, stirring several times. Spread nuts on waxed paper, avoid having them touch, and cool. Makes 2 to 3 cups.

Spiced Nuts

2 c whole almonds
2 c blanched peanuts
2 c sugar
½ c butter or margarine
3 tsp pumpkin pie spice

1 tsp allspice
1 tsp cinnamon
1 tsp ginger
1 tsp salt

Combine all ingredients in an electric skillet. Cook approximately 15 minutes over medium heat or at 350°, stirring and coating the nuts constantly until the sugar is melted and golden brown. Spread nuts in a thin layer onto a waxed paper or foil-lined cookie sheet to cool. Break into clusters.

Mocha Walnuts

½ c granulated sugar
½ c brown sugar,
   firmly packed
½ c sour cream
1 tbsp instant coffee

½ tsp ground
   cinnamon
¼ tsp ground nutmeg
1 tsp vanilla
3 c walnut halves

In a large saucepan, combine first 6 items, mixing well. Cook over medium heat, stirring constantly, to soft ball stage (238°). Remove from heat and stir in vanilla. Add nuts, stirring to coat. Spread onto a buttered baking sheet. Cool and break into pieces. Store in airtight container. Makes about 3½ cups nuts.

Hot Fudge Sauce

12 oz can evaporated milk   1½ c white sugar
12 oz semisweet   1 tsp butter
   chocolate chips   1 tsp vanilla

In a large saucepan, heat milk, chips, and sugar to boiling over medium heat, stirring constantly. Remove from heat. Stir in butter and vanilla. Serve warm over ice cream. Store tightly covered in refrigerator up to 4 weeks. Makes 3 cups.

Easy Apple Butter

5½ lbs apples, peeled
   and finely chopped
4 c sugar

¼ tsp ground cloves
¼ tsp salt
3 tsp cinnamon

Place apples in a Crock-Pot. Combine sugar, cloves, salt, and cinnamon. Pour the seasoning over the apples and mix well. Cover and cook on high for 1 hour. Reduce heat to low; cook for 9–11 hours or until the mixture thickens and is dark brown, stirring occasionally (stir more frequently as it thickens to prevent sticking). Uncover and cook on low 1 hour longer. If desired, stir with a wire whisk until smooth. Spoon into freezer containers, leaving ½-inch headspace. Cover and refrigerate, or freeze, or can in hot water bath. Enjoy the fragrance in the house as this cooks!

Butter Blends

1 c (2 sticks) of butter or margarine, softened

Beat with one of the following groups of ingredients:

Herb: ¼ to ½ cup chopped fresh or 1–2 tablespoons dried herb
    (basil, chives, oregano, savory, tarragon, or thyme), 1 tablespoon
    lemon juice, and ¼ teaspoon salt

Garlic: 2 teaspoons paprika, ½ teaspoon pepper, and 8 cloves
    crushed garlic

Almond: 2 tablespoons finely chopped almonds and 1 teaspoon almond extract

Raspberry: 1 cup crushed raspberries and 2 tablespoons sugar or ½ cup raspberry jam

Orange: 2 teaspoons grated orange peel and 2 tablespoons orange juice

Refrigerate in tightly covered container up to 3 weeks or freeze up to 2 months. Delicious with breads, even with vegetables and meats.

Herb Shake

2 tsp garlic powder
2 tsp onion powder
2 tsp paprika
2 tsp white pepper

2 tsp dry mustard
1 tsp powdered thyme
1 tsp ground celery
   seed

Blend the herbs and store in a shaker. Great way to add taste to salads, meat, poultry, and vegetables.

Homemade Herb Vinegar

2 c white wine vinegar
½ c firmly packed fresh herb (basil, chives, dill weed, mint,
    oregano, rosemary, or tarragon)

Shake vinegar and the herb of your choice in a sealed glass jar. Allow
to stand in a cool, dry place for 10 days. Strain the vinegar. Place 1
sprig of fresh herb of the same variety in a decorative jar or bottle and
add strained vinegar.

Can substitute these for the herb: 6 cloves of garlic or ½ cup chopped
peeled gingerroot.

Homemade Fruit Vinegar

3 c white wine vinegar
2 tbsp honey
2 c of crushed berry like raspberry, blueberry, or cranberry
  (frozen or fresh) or ¼ c lemon or orange rind, shredded

Combine in large saucepan and cover. Bring to a boil, then remove from heat and let stand until cooled. Strain the fruit or rind out. Pour into bottle(s) and seal tightly. Allow to stand at least 24 hours before adding some decorative fruit or rind to the vinegar. Seal tightly. Store at room temperature. Good for approximately 3 months.

Vinegars can be used on salads and vegetables or as marinade for meat, poultry, or fish. The bottles are pretty given unwrapped, just add a touch of ribbon or raffia to the neck.

Homemade Oil

1 c walnuts, almonds, or
    hazelnuts

2 c vegetable oil

Combine nuts and ½ cup oil in blender until nuts are finely chopped. Put nut mixture and remaining oil in a glass container. Cover tightly and allow to stand in a cool, dry place for 10 days. Strain the oil. Store in the refrigerator in a sealed glass bottle. Lasts up to 3 months. Use to accent salads and meats.

Jar Cakes

Bake a cake in a sterilized, 12-ounce, wide-mouthed canning jar. Any quick bread recipe will work, and one recipe stretches over approximately 6 jars. The cake should not bake and rise to more than ¼ to ½ inch from the jar lip. Wipe any drips from the sides. Bake one jar alone first, and gauge how much batter is right. Also gauge appropriate baking time as it can vary as much as 25 to 40 minutes. Record the figures on your recipe for the future. If you have multiple jars in the oven, move the jars during the baking process to encourage even baking. Use heavy mitts to handle the hot jars. Cover with new, boil-prepared lid and ring seal while cake is still hot. The heat should seal them. May store in a cool, dark place up to 3 months. The bread is safe to use as long as the vacuum seal holds and no mold growth appears. The jar cakes serve 1–2 people and remain very moist.

Brownie Jar Cake

2 sterilized 12-oz
   canning jars
1 c flour
1 c sugar
½ tsp baking soda
¼ tsp cinnamon
   (optional)
⅓ c butter or margarine

¼ c water
3 tbsp cocoa
¼ c buttermilk
1 egg, beaten
½ tsp vanilla
¼ c walnuts, finely
   chopped

Brush melted shortening on the inside walls of sterilized jars. (Do not spray with oil or use butter.) In a small bowl, blend flour, sugar, baking soda, and cinnamon. Set aside. In a medium saucepan, combine butter, water, and cocoa. Heat over low and stir until butter melts and mixture is well blended. Remove from heat and stir in the dry mixture. Add buttermilk, egg, and vanilla. Beat by hand until smooth. Fold in nuts. Pour equally into prepared jars. Place jars on a cookie sheet in 325° oven for 35–40 minutes or until a pick inserted deep into the cake comes out clean. Remove from the oven and immediately place a hot lid onto the jars and hold snug with a ring.

Gingerbread Jar Cake

5 sterilized 12-oz canning jars
2¼ c flour
¾ c sugar
1 tsp baking soda
½ tsp baking powder
¼ tsp salt

2 tsp ginger
1 tsp cinnamon
½ tsp ground cloves
¾ c margarine, softened
¾ c water
½ c molasses

Brush melted shortening on the inside walls of sterilized jars. (Do not spray with oil or use butter.) In a large bowl, combine dry ingredients. Stir in margarine, water, and molasses. Divide batter equally among the 5 jars (they should be about half full). Place jars on a cookie sheet in 325° oven for 35–40 minutes or until a pick inserted deep into the cake comes out clean. Remove from the oven and immediately place a hot lid onto the jars and hold snug with a ring.

Pumpkin Spice Jar Cake

8 sterilized 12-oz
    canning jars
1 c raisins, coarsely chopped
1 c walnuts, coarsely chopped
2 c flour
2 tsp baking soda
¼ tsp baking powder
½ tsp salt

2 tsp ground cloves
2 tsp cinnamon
1 tsp ginger
4 large eggs
2 c sugar
1 c oil
16 oz pumpkin (not pie
    filling)

Sterilize jars, and when cooled, brush melted shortening on the inside walls. (Do not spray with oil or use butter.) Combine raisins and walnuts; set aside. Sift dry ingredients together in a large bowl. Add raisins and walnuts; set aside. In another large bowl, beat eggs at high speed 2–3 minutes until thick and yellow. Gradually beat in sugar until thick and light in color. At low speed, beat in oil and pumpkin until well blended. Divide batter among the 8 jars (should be slightly less than half full). Place jars on a cookie sheet in 325° oven for 35–40 minutes or until a pick inserted deep into the cake comes out clean. Remove from the oven and immediately place a hot lid onto the jars and hold snug with a ring.

Frozen Cookie Dough

This year give those short on time (or skill) a gift of cookie dough to bake on those cold, lazy winter evenings after the holiday goodies are gone. Plan to give each person a variety of dough. Use basic recipes for chocolate chip, oatmeal, and peanut butter cookies. Mix up double batches. Put straight into freezer-safe plastic containers or bags. Or, so only what is needed can be baked instead of the whole batch, form the dough into balls and freeze on a cookie sheet. When frozen put them into bags and store in the freezer. Dough will last longer in the freezer than baked cookies, and the recipient will be able to enjoy the cookies warm from the oven. When you give the dough, include a note with baking instructions.

Peach Tea Mix

1 c instant tea mix
1 box peach gelatin

2 c granulated sugar

Combine all ingredients in a large bowl; mix well. Store in an airtight container. To serve, stir about 2 teaspoons of tea mix into 8 ounces of hot water.

Friendship Tea

2 c orange drink mix
2 c sugar
¾ c instant tea mix
¾ tsp ground cloves

¼ oz package of
    lemonade powder
1½ tsp cinnamon

Combine all ingredients and store in airtight container. To brew: Add 3–4 teaspoons tea mix to 1 cup boiling water. Stir until mix completely dissolves.

Friendship Soup Mix in a Jar

½ c dry split peas
⅓ c beef bouillon
   (low sodium)
¼ c pearl barley
½ c dry lentils

¼ c dried minced onion
2 tsp Italian seasoning
½ c uncooked long grain
   brown rice
½ c alphabet macaroni

In a 1½-pint or 1-quart jar, layer the eight ingredients in the order listed. Seal tightly. (If ingredients do not come right up to the top of the jar, you can place a crumpled piece of plastic wrap on top of the last layer to keep layers from shifting.) Store in a cool, dry place until ready to use.

INSTRUCTION CARD:

To prepare soup, you'll need one pound of lean ground beef and a 28-ounce can of diced tomatoes. Remove macaroni from top of jar and set aside. In a large saucepan or Dutch oven, brown beef and drain. Add 3 quarts of water, tomatoes with juice, and soup mix, then bring to a boil. Reduce heat and cover. Simmer for 45 minutes. Add the reserved macaroni and cover. Simmer for 15–20 minutes or until macaroni, peas, lentils, and barley are tender. Yield: 1 batch serves 16.

Spicy Chili Seasoning Mix in a Jar

4 tbsp chili powder
2½ tsp ground coriander
2½ tsp ground cumin

1½ tsp garlic powder
1 tsp dried oregano
½ tsp cayenne pepper

Mix the above and place in a jelly jar. Makes 20 teaspoons of mix or 4 batches of chili.

INSTRUCTION CARD:
Brown 2 pounds lean ground beef and 1 medium chopped onion. Blend in 3 teaspoons chili seasoning. Add a 28-ounce can of tomatoes and 2 15-ounce cans of chili beans. Simmer 40–50 minutes.

Mexican Dip Mix in a Jar

½ c dried parsley
⅓ c dried minced onion
¼ c dried chives

⅓ c chili powder
¼ c ground cumin
¼ c salt

In a large bowl, combine the spices and store in an airtight container. This dip mix can be given in a small sombrero.

INSTRUCTION CARD:

3 tbsp dip mix
1 c mayonnaise (may use low-fat)

1 c sour cream or low-fat plain yogurt

In a medium mixing bowl combine ingredients. Whisk the mixture until smooth. Refrigerate for 2 to 4 hours. Serve with tortilla chips or fresh vegetables. Makes 2 cups.

Cobbler Mix in a Jar

1 c all-purpose flour   1 c sugar
1 tsp baking powder   1 tsp powdered vanilla

Combine and blend the ingredients in a small bowl. Store in an airtight container.

INSTRUCTION CARD:
Serves 8 to 10

4 c fresh or frozen berries
    (blueberries, raspberries, or
    blackberries)
¼ c orange juice
¼ c sugar

1 tsp cinnamon
1 c butter, melted
1 egg
1 jar cobbler mix

Preheat oven to 375°. In large mixing bowl, combine berries, juice, sugar, and cinnamon. Place berries in a 9x13-inch pan. In small mixing bowl, blend the butter with the egg. Add the cobbler mix and stir until the mixture sticks together. Drop the dough by tablespoonfuls on top of the berry filling. Bake for 35–45 minutes or until the topping is golden brown and the filling is bubbling. Allow to cool for 15 minutes before serving.

Fudge Brownie Mix in Jar

2 c sugar
1 c cocoa (not Dutch
   process)

1 c all-purpose flour
1 c chopped pecans
1 c chocolate chips

Mix all the ingredients together and store in an airtight container.

INSTRUCTION CARD:
Makes 24

1 c butter or margarine,
   softened

4 eggs
1 jar fudge brownie mix

Preheat the oven to 325°. Grease a 9x13-inch pan. In a large bowl, cream the butter with a mixer. Add the eggs, one at a time, beating well. Add the brownie mix and continue to beat the mixture until it is smooth. Spread into the greased pan and bake for 40–50 minutes.

Blonde Brownie Mix in a Jar

16 oz brown sugar $\frac{1}{2}$ c chopped pecans
2 c all purpose flour

Combine ingredients. Store in a jar or heavy plastic bag.

INSTRUCTION CARD:
Combine mix with 4 eggs and blend well. Pour into a greased 9x13-inch pan. Bake at 350° for 25–28 minutes.

Candy Cookie Mix in a Jar

½ c sugar
½ c brown sugar,
   firmly packed

1 tsp powdered vanilla
1 tsp baking soda
2 c flour

Combine all ingredients in a medium bowl. Whisk the ingredients together until they are evenly distributed, making sure all brown sugar lumps are crushed. Store in an airtight jar.

INSTRUCTION CARD:
Makes 3 dozen cookies

1 c unsalted butter or
  margarine, softened
1 c candy bar chunks (Reese's peanut
  butter cups, Butterfinger bars,
  white or milk chocolate chunks)

1 large egg
1 jar candy cookie mix

Preheat oven to 350°. In a large bowl, beat the butter with a mixer until it is smooth. Add the egg, and continue beating until the egg is well blended. Add the cookie mix and candy bar chunks and blend on low. Form the cookies into 1½-inch balls and place them 2 inches apart on an ungreased cookie sheet. Bake for 10–12 minutes, until golden on the edges. Remove from oven and cool on cookie sheet for 2 minutes.

Magic Cookie Bar Mix in a Jar

¼ c walnuts, chopped
1 c butterscotch chips
1 c semisweet
   chocolate chips

½ c shredded coconut
1 c graham crackers,
   crushed

Combine ingredients in a wide-mouth glass canning jar by order listed above.

INSTRUCTION CARD:

Preheat oven to 350°. Add ½ cup melted butter to graham crackers. Place in a 9x9-inch baking pan and pat to evenly cover the bottom. Scatter remaining ingredients on top. Pour a 14-ounce can of sweetened condensed milk evenly over everything. Bake for 30 minutes.

Snickerdoodle Mix in a Jar

2¾ c all purpose flour
¼ tsp salt
1 tsp baking soda

2 tsp cream of tartar
1½ c sugar

In a large bowl, combine the ingredients with a whisk. Store the mix in an airtight container.

INSTRUCTION CARD:
Makes about 5 dozen cookies

1 c butter or margarine,
softened
2 eggs

1 jar Snickerdoodle mix
½ c sugar
1 tbsp cinnamon

Preheat oven to 350°. In a large bowl, use an electric mixer to cream the butter until fluffy. Add the eggs and beat on low speed until the mixture is smooth. Add the mix and continue to beat on low speed until the dough begins to form. Shape the dough into 1-inch balls and roll in a blend of the cinnamon and sugar. Arrange on ungreased baking sheets 2 inches apart and bake for 16–19 minutes, or until light tan. Place on wire racks to cool.

Dog Biscuit Mix in a Jar

1 c all-purpose unbleached
   flour
1 c whole wheat flour
½ c yellow cornmeal
½ tsp garlic powder

½ c instant nonfat dry
   milk powder
1 tsp brown sugar or
   white sugar
Pinch of salt

In a medium mixing bowl, combine all ingredients. Pour into a 1-quart, wide-mouth canning jar. Close jar tightly. Tie a dog biscuit cookie cutter and instruction card around the top of the jar with a pretty ribbon.

INSTRUCTION CARD:

Position a rack in the center of the oven. Preheat to 250°. Place contents of the jar in a medium sized bowl. Add one large egg, ½ cup shredded sharp cheddar cheese, ¼ cup grated Parmesan cheese, ¼ to ½ cup hot chicken broth, beef broth, or very hot water.

Make very heavy, but not sticky, dough. Add more flour or water, a spoonful at a time if dough is too moist (use flour) or too dry (use hot water).

Turn out dough onto a floured pastry cloth and knead 8–10 times until elastic. Let dough rest for 5 minutes. Roll out dough ½-inch thick and cut with a dog-bone shaped cutter. Place cookies close together. They will not spread.

Bake for 1 hour, rotate the baking trays in the oven (turn tray around 180 degrees), and bake them another half hour. Cool the cookies in the pan for 1 minute, then transfer to a wire cake rack to cool completely.

Gift Bundles

*"Each man should give what he has decided in his heart to give,
not reluctantly or under compulsion,
for God loves a cheerful giver."*

2 CORINTHIANS 9:7

Fill an inexpensive basket or other container with a variety
of items that will be meaningful to a special person.

FOR TEA TIME: A teacup. A teapot. Strainer. A variety of teas. A small jar of honey. Homemade jams or jellies with crackers or a small loaf of homemade bread. Shortbread cookies. Tea stirrers.

FOR BATH TIME: Bath salts. Scented soaps and lotions. Sponge. Scented candle. Washcloths. Chocolate truffles. A doorknob sign that says "Pampering. Do Not Disturb."

FOR FAMILY NIGHT: A family-friendly movie on VHS or DVD or a gift certificate to a video rental store. Two bags of microwave popcorn. Theater-sized boxes of candy. Kool-Aid mix in envelopes or 4 cans of soda pop.

FOR THE GARDENER: Small hand tools (spade, trowel, rake, and cutters). Gloves. Knee pads. Plant markers. Seed packets. Bulbs. Bonemeal or other multipurpose fertilizer. (Place things in a bucket or watering can.)

FOR THE BIRDWATCHER: Bird feeder. A bag of seed. Suet with cage. Bird guidebook. Rain gauge. Outdoor thermometer.

FOR THE DO-IT-YOURSELF PERSON: Tape measure. Hammer. Screwdriver with changeable heads. Variety box of nails and screws. Small level. Tool apron. Utility knife. Safety glasses. Superglue. Duct tape. How-to book.

FOR THE WRITER: Stationery. Pens. Envelopes. Stamps. Postcards. Address book (with some special addresses already included).

FOR THE TEACHER: Colorful pencils. Erasers. Post-it notepads. Packets of stickers. Red pens. Highlighters.

FOR THE STUDENT: Calculator. Notebooks. Pencils, pens, and highlighters. Study lamp. Dictionary and thesaurus. Post-it notepads in various sizes.

FOR THE NEW MOM: A large bottle of pain reliever. Hand lotion. A picture frame. A brag book. A CD of favorite lullabies. Chocolate. Coffee. Coupons promising your baby-sitting services.

FOR THE BABY: A boo-boo bunny. First Christmas ornament. Containers of powder, baby lotion, baby wash or shampoo, diaper rash ointment, and baby wipes. Washcloths. Burping clothes. Receiving blankets. A teething ring. Pacifier. Bib. Night light. (Place in a diaper bag or small waste can.)

FOR THE COOK: Measuring spoons and cups. Spices. Apron. Kitchen timer. Recipe box or other organizer. Cookbook. Small mixing bowls. Whisk. Box of storage bags. (Use a large mixing bowl or colander lined with a dish towel to hold things.)

FOR THE OUTDOOR CHEF: Barbecue tools. Aluminum foil. Lighter fluid. Apron. Citronella candles. Bug spray. (Place everything in a cooler.)

FOR THE BOOK LOVER: Two or three new books. Small reading lamp. Bookmark. Packets of coffee or tea. Cookies.

FOR THE CHOCOLATE LOVER: A package of candy bars. Brownies with fudge icing. Truffles. German chocolate cake. Several variations of fudge. Chocolate syrup. A couple packages of chocolate pudding mix. Chocolate covered pretzels. Chocolate/fudge butter cookies. Hot chocolate mix.

FOR THE CAR LOVER: A steering wheel cover. An ice scraper. A sun shade. A fire extinguisher. Some silly fuzzy dice. An air freshener. A bottle of car wash, tire cleaner, spot remover, and car wax. A buffer cloth. (Use a bucket to hold everything.)

FOR THE SPORTS LOVER: A sports blunders video. Small game balls. A pack of trading cards. Ball cap.

FOR THE COFFEE LOVER: A special coffee cup. A variety of small packets of flavored coffee. Small jar of creamer (also available in flavors). Bean grinder. Chocolate-dipped cinnamon sticks or spoons. Butter cookies.

FOR THE PET LOVER: A ball. Squeak toys. Chews. Treats. Book on pet care. Collar, leash, and name tag. Bowl with pet's name on it.

The Wrap Up

*"The Lord Jesus himself said:
'It is more blessed to give than to receive.'"*

ACTS 20:35

Design Your Own Gift Wrap!

Be creative by combining and designing with the following:

Brown packing paper or white butcher paper or even large brown paper grocery bags
Rubber stamps and ink
Stickers

Paint
Design tools (sponge, cotton balls, toothbrush, old pot scrubber, straw to blow paint)

Alternative Papers

Who says you have to use only Christmas-printed papers?

- Try using leftover wallpaper or shelf paper.
- Paper with your child's drawings from school, old maps, newspaper, and the comics.
- Wrap a box with plain paper and glue old Christmas cards to the sides.
- Even aluminum foil and colored plastic wrap will work.

Reusable Wraps

As an alternative to store-bought paper that can get expensive, try wrapping a box in something that can be reused by the recipient.

Bandana or scarf
Blanket
Fabric
Laundry bag

Pillowcase
Tablecloth
Towel
Tulle, netting, or lace

Window Box

Cut one or more designs in the lid of a shoebox, copier paper box, or other box with solid lid. Wrap the box with paper, trimming flush with the cutout. Tape plastic wrap (clear or colored) over the cutout on the inside of the box. Let your gift peek through.

Window Bag

Cut a design out on one side of a sturdy bag. Cover the cutout on the inside with clear or colored plastic wrap. Fill the bag, then fold the top over, letting a hint of the contents show through. With a hole punch, put two holes at least 1 inch apart in the top fold. Put ribbon, raffia, or yarn through the holes and tie a bow that hangs above the window.

Fabric Gift Bags

Cut a 16x19-inch rectangle of holiday fabric for each bag. Lay a 2-foot piece of narrow cord or ribbon along the 19-inch side and turn 1 inch of fabric over the cord, wrong sides facing. Stitch ¼ inch from the edge. Fold the 16-inch sides together with right sides facing. Stitch a ½-inch seam around the 3 rough sides. Trim the corners, and turn right side out.

SHORTCUT:
Cut 2 pieces of calico, flannel, or felt with pinking shears to 9x12 inches. With wrong sides facing, sew ½-inch seam. (You could hand sew it with embroidery floss.) Fill the bag with a small gift, gather the top closed, and secure with a ribbon or raffia bow.

Fabric Envelopes

To make a fabric envelope that will measure 5x8 inches, cut a piece of holiday fabric 8x13 inches with pinking shears. Measure 3 inches up the long side and mark it with a pin (you'll have a 3-inch flap). Fold the 8-inch end up to the pin (wrong sides facing) so that your pouch area will be 5 inches deep. Sew a ½-inch seam around the 3 sides of the pouch area. ¾-inch from the unsewn edge of the flap, cut a small slit in the center of the flap. Lay the flap over the pouch and mark where the slit touches the pouch. Fold a 6-8-inch piece of ¼-inch ribbon in half, and at the fold, hand sew it onto the pouch at the mark. Fill your pouch with the gift, fold flap over, and secure with ribbon.

Tag It

- Print free gift tag designs from the Internet.
- Print your own tag design onto a sheet of computer labels.
- Simply fold a rectangular piece of matching wrapping paper in half for a little card tag.
- Use a bookmark or other card with sentiment that you can write the name on.
- Buy a key chain, ink pen, magnet, jewelry pin, or other item with the recipient's name preprinted on it.

Ornament Tags

Buy inexpensive, plain-colored ornaments with matte finish. Use a pointed, permanent marker to write the recipient's name.

Shipping Cookies

Bar cookies and drop cookies like plain chocolate chip and peanut butter travel best. Frosted and filled cookies may soften and stick together. Cool cookies completely before packing. Carefully pack the cookies between layers of waxed paper in a tin, empty coffee can, or rigid box. Pack a piece of apple or slice of bread with soft cookies to keep them fresh. Use crumpled waxed paper or plain popcorn to fill in any open space. There should be no room for the cookies to shift. Pack this tin in a larger, sturdy shipping box. Pad the area around the tin with crumpled paper or other packing material, seal, and address. Write "perishable" on the box.